# THE FREEDOM OF HISTORY

# THE FREEDOM
# OF HISTORY

*Poems by*

## JIM MOORE

MILKWEED EDITIONS

THE FREEDOM OF HISTORY
Poems by Jim Moore

91  90  89  88      4  3  2  1

Published by *Milkweed Editions*
Post Office Box 3226
Minneapolis, Minnesota 55403
*Books may be ordered from the address above*

Cover Photograph by JoAnn Verburg © 1988

Library of Congress Catalog Card Number: 88-42975
ISBN 0-915943-32-8

Publication of this book is supported in part by grants from The Litera-
ture Program of the National Endowment for the Arts, The Dayton
Hudson Foundation for Dayton's and Target Stores, The First Bank
System Foundation, the Jerome Foundation, the Metropolitan Regional
Arts Council from funds appropriated by the Minnesota State Legisla-
ture, with special assistance from the McKnight Foundation, the Arts
Development Fund of United Arts, and by contributions from many
generous individuals, corporations, and foundations.

The author wishes to thank the editors of the following magazines in
which some of these poems first appeared: *The American Poetry Review*,
*The Antioch Review*, *Ironwood*, *Momentum Magazine*, *Paris Review*, *Seneca
Review*, and *Sonora Review*. "The Valley Called Curve", "Winter Smoke",
and "Snow" were first published in *The Kenyon Review*—New Series,
Winter 1981 (1982). Volume 3, No. 1, Volume 4, No. 1. "Instead of Fea-
tures" was first published in *The Poet Dreaming In The Artist's House*,
Milkweed Editions, 1984.

*For JoAnn Verburg*

# ACKNOWLEDGEMENTS

*This book has been twelve years in the making and a number of writers and editors have made all the difference along the way. I want to thank Jill Breckenridge, Don Brunnquell, Emilie Buchwald, Marisha Chamberlain, Carol Conroy, Patricia Hampl, Phebe Hanson, Margaret Hasse, Margot Kriel Galt, Lewis Hyde, Deborah Keenan, Patricia Kirkpatrick, Miriam Levine, Bill Mohr, David Mura, Wendy Salinger, and Bart Schneider.*

*I want to thank The Bush Foundation and The Minnesota State Arts Board for grants that helped give me time to work and the means to travel which, in turn, led to more work. I also want to thank The Loft, an organization which, through its Loft-McKnight grant, provided financial support and which, through classes, readings, and many other activities, has become an invaluable part of my life as a writer.*

*And finally, I particularly want to thank my family: my wife, JoAnn Verburg; my sister, Madeline Moore; my niece, Mira Moore; and my mother and father.*

# TABLE OF CONTENTS

# THE FREEDOM OF HISTORY

# I
## Today's Meditation

Today's Meditation:
## "IT'S NOT SUPPOSED TO LAST FOREVER"
Cavafy

Every day, and for no apparent reason,
I remember prison. My footlocker,
barbed wire out the window, how coffee tasted—
instant, lukewarm from the bathroom tap
first thing in the morning. I would stand there
sipping, watching the Standard sign through barred windows,
miles down the road. I can still see how red
that sign was in the pale sky at dawn,
how beautiful it seemed to me, so far away
beyond the fence, and yet near somehow.
I stood next to the shaving mirror,
as close to the sky as I could get.
Even then, I knew how lucky I was
"and I really lived in undivided love," as Cavafy says.
I understood how the loneliness and the love
would always be mixed up inside me,
like a sky and its Standard sign bound
together in the little nearness of time.

Today's Meditation:
*HAPPINESS*

In the end,
all that matters is light and dark,
and what's not finished between them.
As long as he stands back far enough, deeply
enough inside the room, he is fine, he gets
the point of things: how they come, then must go.
But the blue sea beyond the window: it has
always done this to him, always forced him
further into happiness than he thought he could stand to go.

## TODAY'S MEDITATION

He went to bed early, and dreamed well.
Wild sex, many secret meetings.
Towards dawn, he woke as usual.
That is, he felt somehow guilty
for the pleasures, the dark secrets.
He noticed the leaves, and took heart.
They, too, had had a wild night.
They were yellow and shrivelled, barely
hanging on. As if they also had loved furiously
and secretly, and now were in a state
of shock. It was a new day, and all
over his country men and women were making coffee,
putting on the shirts and pants behind which our bodies
lie still all day, sleeping like owls, worn out
from the night's long chase, its bloody victories
and secret, unremarked defeats.

Today's Meditation:
## *TRAVEL: RAVENNA*

I thought we came here for the mosaics.
But really it was to ride this bus
with an old man on one side who smiled
and an old man on the other who frowned.
Really, we came here to see
the yes and the no creased across the stubble
on two mens' faces: the one way
a life of ecstasy,
one way a life of absolute denial.

Here in Ravenna where a mighty empire
began and ended near the sea,
two mighty camps
still meet daily on the bus,
the empire of yes and the empire of no.

Nearby the mosaics shine with the impersonal delight
of those whose lives have been resolved as art,
their dark-rimmed eyes already inducted
into eternity: so far away can the yes and no go, so
beautifully can the empire be shaped
into cut and glittering stones.

This, then, is our present: to chart
the past— obscured, dense—
already ascended into the heaven
of finished things. Meanwhile,
the yes and the no make themselves at home inside us,

relay their secret messages back and forth
like children who refuse to be silent
at a funeral, death so near they could
reach out and touch it, but life— its thousand
urgencies that must be whispered *now*—
even nearer.

Today's Meditation:

## A SUMMER AFTERNOON, VENICE

You feel how good it is,
this earth, sitting on the cool bridge
made of shadows
that swings between pine tree and church.

Pigeons search through the dry grass,
diligent, working their turf.
If, at 44, you begin to learn
you are not, after all, the point of the world,

what then? The bells ring 6 pm,
the shadows no longer just a bridge,
but a road widening into darkness
and the night beyond. Everyone

is going for a walk on that road
one time soon, if not here
where the roads are made of water,
then somewhere else, somewhere equally strange,

some tide-lulled Venice of the brain.
There is a moment when our empires fade to nothing at last.
Where once we had stood ashamed,
unable to understand our place in the universe,

now moonlight is there, shining its bridge across the open water.

Today's Meditation:

## THE CRUCIFIXION
### (Tintoretto)

It's still going on.
It's not even close to being over:
the man in pain goes on hanging there, he
hasn't got a prayer. He'll go slowly,
he'll take hours. This isn't
about God, it's anyone who's going down
inch by inch and won't be coming back again:
there's not a thing we can do to stop it.
For centuries, this has been happening:
someone dies slowly, alone, without comfort.

No wonder the sky is black behind the dying man,
and the fern turns a sickly green
and the ground is a dusty unforgiving slab
of cracked earth. This is where we live
and the only God to believe in is the God
of Suffering, the man or woman bound hand and foot
on the cross of whatever pain has finally claimed them.

Here's what we do, Tintoretto says, we who live on this earth,
who watch from the sidelines.
Some of us ride fancy horses, pause
a moment, gape in horror, then
gallop away. Some of us are poor,
are on foot. We, too, stare, we, too, leave;
but more slowly, one step at a time,
looking back sometimes, we can't
help ourselves, such suffering. Some of us
point. With our right hand we are saying,

*look*. But our heads are turned away,
we know we need to see what the world
is doing to one of its own, but we can't bear
to really look. Some of us hide
in dark corners: the ones who have cards and dice.
Bottles that are almost empty
guide some of us through the darkness: for us there
is nothing to see, nothing to look at, all suffering
is a distant smear of paint, beautiful in its way.

There are always a few among us who gather
at the foot of suffering. The humble ones,
usually the women, the mothers,
the ones who love not because it is right,
but because they must. In this collapse
of women in beautiful robes next to two men
who believed in him, in this collapse
called grief, in this sorrow
beyond endurance that is —
in the name of love — endured,
in this collapse of the faithful onto bare earth
begins what Tintoretto sees as the only peace
that is worth painting, the one
that lives like this, sprawled at the feet of suffering.

It is the rest of us who sadden Tintoretto:
how busy the painting is with all the ways there are
to miss the point of our lives in the face of such
incessant, unceasing mortalities. There is no justice
such suffering could possibly serve. And far in the background,

one ghostly figure standing by herself
on the left, surely a signature
to all the rest, a pure creature
of imagination, solitary in her flickering,
insubstantial body, blessed
by the absence of life, the absence of death.

# II
## The Freedom of History

# THE FREEDOM OF HISTORY

I

*It is a spring night in Prague. A man in a park in his mid-thirties and a woman, twenty years older, are sitting on a bench they've pulled over to a corner. This way they can see the river and the Charles Bridge. She speaks:*

These beads are too big: amber
from some other century when necks
were larger. I think my whole body
must be a sack meant for that century.
I'm six feet of awkwardness and the beads
look like carnations of melting butter on a string.

Don't turn away. I won't talk
about myself now. It's so easy
to feel sorry for yourself with a man
who listens as you do: your whole body
leans toward me and my English
is a secret between us. I have no one
but the children to speak it with now.

Everything you hear in Prague is music
because you can't understand our language.
It is a wide river that washes slowly around you. Or,
(how I love metaphor at night
with the chestnuts in bloom and the blue
electrical flicks of the trams across the river;
and you inside that white shirt)
you stand on the bank of a strange music:
the language reminds you of nothing
but a waterfall, a pillow of sound . . .

No, don't turn away. I won't talk about you.
I know you came here to forget
how to explain your life. We drank
a toast to that in white Moravian wine,
though the Germans
at the next table were so loud we had to shout it.

I'll explain history
the way the city taught me.
But wait. Did you hear that?
An owl. The first I've heard in years here.
It must be by the old water wheel over there.
I love creatures. Now that they let me translate
from English again, I do books
by veterinarians about the pets
they've restored to health. That owl
is wild. I must tell
my daughter. She'll want to name him
something human and pretend, she, too,
wakes up at night and watches the city
with feathers at her sides.

This is the city at the center of everything.
(White blossoms of the horse chestnut
fall in your hair.)
Europe runs us through in every direction.
We have no ocean, no horizon
we can look into endlessly. We have
no distance to lose ourselves in.
For centuries we have built this city
to be our ocean. This is why the buildings
peel in pink layers of stone:
they are waves slowly finding a shore
in the century before them, beneath them

in the layer before their own. You know
the silence old people drift in and out of.
Attention bores them. They'd rather
open a door into a courtyard and see
a girl standing in sunlight: she holds a brown pitcher
filled with beer brought from the corner
for her father. Or, they'd rather turn and twist
and be a narrow road winding up a hill
toward a magnificent castle, black and shadowy
against the blue powder of a spring day.

You've said the city pulls you
and you don't know why. I want to read you
what my husband wrote when he first came to Prague.
It was fifteen years ago. Things were different then.
There was a sort of freedom. (You don't
have to look around: it's safe.
We look innocuous, like lovers.
No one would guess that what we say
might matter.)

You are wrong to turn away like that.
I'm not talking about me. This is him,
like you, a stranger. He, too, was sick
of himself, of all the questions, the decisions
to make that never seemed to matter. He, too,
wanted an oracle. Like you, he came here on impulse.
Those ornate combs he gave me for my hair:
they were meant to turn me regal:
piles of hair and a determined chin! Anyway,
he was young then, too: and English
to his toes. He came here to meet my mother,
to see the city where we might live

and learn to translate one another's languages.

I brought the first letter he wrote after he left:

"Prague is like a dream, more so than any other city I've seen. It's so odd and so filled with that old life. Archaic— suddenly that word, its arch-like sound, takes on life. The arches of the archaic.

"Prague is not a museum, not an artificial arrangement of fragments from a culture. It is a whole; people live there. The city has a life of its own, separate from any one individual's life. It all grew so slowly, it all moves so slowly now. It is not a city geared to efficiency or to a known goal; but to a journey that can only occur in streets that twist under arches.

"It is a city built before capitalism and through a strange twist of fate still preserved from it. There is little 'exchange' there; much drifting and wandering. Its solitude overarches one's own. It is not a city desperate for the personal exchange, whether of money or relationship. Things take their course. You wander. The city catches you up, just as a dream does. There are no companions when you dream, you always do it alone. It is a city which grows in power at night. Far from feeling excluded at night as you do in any large city in the west if you are alone— exchange grows even more desperate in London at night— you feel even more embraced, more included. The dream grows more vivid.

"I'm not being romantic; it's worse than that and more dangerous: it's a-moral. It's a-contemporary. The city of Prague is a kind of music, the only art which represents nothing but itself. It is a world that will be endangered the more often I come to Prague. It is a world that will end entirely when I learn the language: the more I understand the 'real' Prague, the less music I will hear."

When we lived in London for a year
I loved the tube most.
Late at night, the smell of cinders
and stale electricity. The buckets
of sand. And the old men
who wait for the last train.
Have you seen how they look
straight ahead at the wall of the tunnel
opposite them? (I am too elegant in this dress.
It's so long, so green, puffy in the sleeves
like a mushroom rotting in the bin. I wore it
for you. Because you're from New York.
I should have known it was wrong:
elegance, even out of date,
is not what you came for.) They wear
thick coats, the tweed is smudged,
their hats . . . anyway, it's late in the tube
and the posters have begun to peel.
The tunnels seem ancient then, burrowed
into a mountainside. It is quiet.
London seems miles away. It is the closest thing
London has to silence, to the arches,
to the centuries that have hollowed themselves out
into Prague.
All of the west is one big shop.
There is nothing for you to do but make decisions.
Prague is a city
without decisions; without choice; the centuries
tell us how to be silent; the state
tells us how to speak. But I've said it wrong.
Inside the silence, an owl hoots:
it makes me want to ride the broken water wheel
round and round in the silent night.

*She stops speaking. They both get up from the bench and walk to the low
wall that separates the park from the river. It is very late now. The smell
of horse chestnut blossoms is everywhere: that strange mixture of freshness
and rotting. He wants to be alone. They agree to meet two nights from
then in the Slavia. Her high heels— somehow she manages to walk in
them as if they were boots— slap loudly on the cement. He looks for a
moon, but can't see one.*

2

*The Slavia is a cavernous old coffee house. It faces the river almost oppo-
site from the Kampa. They sit at a table facing the Hradcany, the castle
which dominates Prague. It is lit up. All around them people smoke,
drink coffee, talk, and read the newspapers. She speaks:*

> So, you came. You want
> to hear more. But first,
> look around you. What bird
> do the people here remind you of?
> I see the dove everywhere I look:
> so much gray in the jackets,
> in the felt hats and sweaters.
> So much bending and cooing,
> poking at cakes, whispers, gossip.
> Sometimes I think we'll all grow wings
> and fly into the past. Live in a belfry
> or on the edge of a flying buttress
> from one of those centuries
> that you have come here to rediscover;
> maybe you and I will be doves together . . .
> but I forget; you say
> you've had enough of metaphor:
> you want the truth.

Have you noticed how the centuries collide?
Romanesque, gothic, baroque; they never stop
running into each other. And yet,
when a person walks, say Karlova Street,
it's impossible not to feel it as logical
as a bed-time story a father tells his children,
a fairy tale in which everything belongs:
owls in water wheels, horse chestnuts
blooming in a man's hair, a woman
whose husband died in a crash in London.

Forgive me for being personal.
I can't help my life. It collides, too:
our own century and our lives. The truth
you want is lying under stone.
The Jewish Cemetery.
It's so old
no one has been buried there for hundreds of years.
The graves have all collided;
stone is stacked on stone.
They buried their dead in layers,
century after century. Now the stones
are dug up, so many you can hardly walk
from grave to grave. These stones
are the new grass, the meadows
where this century has learned to graze.
Isn't death our architecture?

So, you see now, I am not alone.
I am a Jew.
My metaphors keep me company.
I don't blame you for wanting
the silence of our streets, the anonymous
architecture of a city that has stood so long

in spite of everything. It's good,
sometimes, to wander like Kafka
in Italy, or you, here. He needed
so much: the sun, the hair
of women. You need . . .

(Don't turn away. I won't tell you
more than you can hear.)

My little girl wants to be an artist.
She likes to draw spires and roofs,
the tops of things. I come home
from work and there she is,
cross-legged on the window-ledge.
She loves to look.
When she's tired at dinner
she watches the grain of the wood
in our table. She's cold
in winter. Here's a poem
someone her age, her race, wrote in '42 at Terezin,
a concentration camp for children:

> " . . . those thirty thousand who are
> sleeping —
> Who shall awake one day
> And shall see their own blood shed around.
>
> "Once I was a child — two years ago.
> My childhood was longing for other worlds.
>
> "But I believe that I'm only sleeping now,
> That I shall return with my childhood one day,

With that childhood like a wild rose,
Like a bell that calls one up from dreams.

"  . . . What a horrible childhood that decides
    for itself
That this one is good and that one is bad!
Far away in the distance my childhood is
    sweetly sleeping
On the paths of the Stromovka Park:

"Perhaps one day I shall realize
That I was only such a tiny creature —
Just as tiny and unimportant
As the whole of that choir —
                those thirty thousand."

He didn't know that choir would reach six million;
for me, they never stop singing.
And I have seen the German tourists
eat their sandwiches sitting on the stones
of the dead in the Jewish Cemetery.
Do you want more truth?
Forgive me my anger, my irony.
It's rare to speak in English,
to find someone so unknown
to history as you are.
Tomorrow, I'll show you
a garden with the mystery
my husband loved. The Slavia
is no place to forgive wounds.
I told my daughter about the owl.
She wants to draw it; but the eyes
stop her: those rings. She keeps

circling in the shadow of his sight.
I wish I hadn't told her.

3

*The afternoon is sunny. They meet at the Waldstein Castle. She guides
him from there to a garden two blocks away. It is on a steep hill and is a
long walk to the top. She speaks as they walk. At the top they find a
bench where they can look over the roofs of the old town and the city.*

Here's where the secret begins,
the space anyone needs who wants
to look at things carefully. Veterinarians
are all the same: they have
their favorites they speak to
repeatedly, but who never answer
in the fawning language of the pet.
Artists, philosophers, priests, veterinarians —
anyone who looks repeatedly at the world
and tries to understand — needs such an animal.
In Prague these secret gardens are our unspeaking
but attentive beasts.

Here's where we sat. My husband
loved the roofs from up above like this.
They have the comfort of a quilt,
the old American ones
that took years to make: jagged squares,
unpredictable, crazy; but held together
by the care and dreamy absorption
of the ones who sewed. From here, from this secret place
that holds us and does not speak,
I see the quilt whole; not separate patches
but the centuries sewn together into the tiles
that cover us all. From here the city

36

always looks asleep under the dazzling haze
of red tiles in sunlight. From here
the city never stops dreaming. Last night
I dreamed you were one of the secret police.
You wouldn't let me photograph my city.
You wore that brown sweater of yours,
only it had turned to armor. You smiled,
then broke my camera. You said,
"Lincoln is my hero,"

Yes, turn away. I don't blame you.
I think you were my husband
trying to return young again
to warn me against the images
I love. It is dangerous to stand
in a secret place and look down on the city
where you live and say of it:

this is a dream. It's dangerous
in the secret place, with the lilacs
and bridal wreath blooming sweet
and acrid. It's too perfect
with the wind on your back
in a high and hidden place. You begin
to see for miles; far beyond the quilt
covering your own life, beyond even
the hundred spires that rise from Prague.

You stand in the secret place and you see
the flood of distance, the shimmer
of the unknown. It never stops, that slow
movement, the third, in Beethoven's *Hammerclavier*.
I saw a Hungarian play it once;
he, too, was beginning to go bald

(no, don't be embarrassed; the head
becomes more powerful then, as well as silly.)
He bent to the keys
as if looking for something
between the smooth ivory fingers. He lifted
his own fingers so slowly: they had become weights
that could barely move through the slabs of ivory
as he looked for what was lost
in that landscape of granite and winter:
flooded fields, bare trees, and the light
that only distance gives to snow.
Have I gone too far?
Isn't this what you wanted:
to be inside the curved panel
of a God's landscape, a smudge
of color far off in the corner
of Monet's largest water-lily?
It was for this that my husband worked
those long nights in London
when the rain is a blanket
unravelling its endless fibers in the yellow light
of streetlamps. Here, too, the nights are long,
distance as impossible to measure as the childhood
of one who dies at birth. Distance, dusk, the owl
that sleeps under the steady eyelashes
of a young girl's careful looking.


4

*She is alone in the vinarna called* The Golden Hat. *She sits at a table
waiting for her food. As she waits, she thinks about the young man who
has left now to return to New York.*

How much I forgot to tell him!
But men are different.

38

It's so easy to bore them.
But I think he would have liked
the cucumbers on the white platter
they always serve here with a little salt.
And the Camembert sprinkled with paprika
and white slivers of sweet onion.
It is always so silent,
the walls thick, curved like the wine cellar
of a monastery centuries ago
when history was a dream,
not a dialectic. But the dream remains
inside the dry Moravian wine. Tourists
don't come here. I've never heard German once.
Only the composer
Smolinik goes out of his way to sit here
drinking wine. All he does
is revise now, old work
from the war years.
It is easy to sit here for hours
with the wine, the cool walls, the silence.
Nothing seems to happen,
as if we were monks sunk in prayer
in the deep dream of a god whose need
for our devotion never stops.
It's almost 3 o'clock. My little artist
will be home soon. Then dinner,
and afterwards that silly book
about the pet beaver to translate.

Later yet, long after the neighborhood sleeps,
I'll walk in the narrow streets beneath the castle.
There'll be a moon tonight. I'll do ten pages,
then walk. I need my city to myself.

I won't let my city regret me.
How many moons I've seen
hang for a moment over the castle wall.
When no one's looking late at night
I pick lilies-of-the-valley
from beneath the castle wall.
Such a tiny flower, such small white bells
to be ringing in the moonlight
beneath all that stone. I don't need him,
that man—I'm not alone—I have my eyes
which don't belong to me, but are two
amazing friends who keep opening for me
onto spires, Camembert, and the moon.
I'm not alone. When a tram car
flickers in the distance anyone sitting
by the window is my friend. He sways
with tiredness and I sway with him;
he turns toward the beautiful woman
two seats over and I understand.
We are always afraid, but never stop looking.

I am alone with all the others:
the ping pong table beneath the frescoes;
a boy leaning his head out the window of a wall
centuries thick to call his friend across the square;
a mother pushing a baby carriage; a grandma
carrying a solitary orange as if it were the sun in a string bag
to her boy, the night porter at the hospital.
I know them all—
the Russian woman no one has spoken to since '69
who puts out her patches of laundry each day
hoping a neighbor will finally take pity and speak;
and the other woman who cries
if even a squirrel should die:

and, oh, the lives of the men
glimpsed through the wooden doors of the smoky taverns.
They stand behind their tall glasses of beer
and look through the golden windows of those half-litres
into longed-for garden paradises filled with fat carrots and
televisions, roses
for their wives in blue jeans and lipstick;
and the cool night air in which no one is screaming.

It is here, in these lives, all of them, that the city
honeycombs the thick centuries with the breath of the living,
with brooms and feather ticks, with buckets
full of soapy water, school satchels and sweat,
until the centuries grow light with the porous breath of life
and are swung up over the backs of the living like so many sacks
of laundry
carried into the future where their clothes will be worn again
shining with the heat of the freshly washed,
put on as if for the first time ever.

# III
## WILD LIGHT

## WINTER SMOKE

white manes of wild light
behind the black branches of the dying elms
that line the street, withered
like amputated limbs
that have been stuck in the ground
so someone will remember to cart them away.

Mane after billowing mane of winter smoke.
The horses are escaping
into the air.
They streak the face of the sky.

As if, simply because we were born
we earned these tears,
this sky, those manes of wild light
galloping away behind the black branches of our dying world.

## SNOW

They are making the world all over.
This time there is the furred breath of snow.
It is silent forever in the new world.
Silent, calm, and falling whitely.
The snow is a breath, like the flutter
of a baby's sleep. It turns this way and that.
The little chest of the world
has no idea what the future might bring.
I am the slow falling.
I rake the world from rooftop to rooftop
and regret nothing in the sharp crystals
of the lost dawn I might have been.
Dropping, dropping,
I am breaking up the sky.
I become the length and breadth,
the unmarked thickness across the windshield.
I am the evenhanded emptiness,
breathing in like the baby asleep in the new ship
of its untried body, breathing out in the shape
of a snow-driven man, still sailing
the white drifts of his own quiet breaking.

## YOU AND SNOW

Like snow, I was born
in the distant belly of a mother
I never knew as well as when,
point by lovely point,
I was forming myself inside her.
I came from nowhere,
fell softly on new air.
I did not know where the drift of weather
or the iron tide of chance would carry me.
I fell far beyond my own control,
giddy with release.
I was most myself
in this my only falling
onto our earth.

Snow's depth is the instant shape
it gives a thing: what snow touches shifts,
just slightly, bringing the sweet pleasure
of merest change,
the way a human will touch a human
lightly on the wrist and that day
is different, slightly and forever:

I am one among many,
our lives linked, as drifting snow
is linked, in mutual need and fallen beauty.

# INTO THE CIRCLE OF DEATH
*Sioux effigy of a dying horse*

Someone believed that death was a flying horse
and carved it in mid-air, leaping. You can see
the love of flesh as it curves in delight around its leap.
Someone worked hard to give death
this blood-stained transparency.

They brought the wounded horses here,
into the circle of death. It was hard
when you had to push a blind horse into the circle
as its own blood rose into its sight.
And if the horse's rider were dead, then a stranger
had to bring the beast to its death. This effigy
is filled with the long body,
leaping; the four hooves complete to the last detail.
They refuse to rest on earth.
The forelegs are stained pink, bloody stockings
pulled over the warm yellow wood of the outstretched body.

The reins are looped over the arched back.
The riderless horse is guided,
the black hairs of the tail tightly bound at their base,
beginning to spread, beginning to open wide.

## IN THE AVIARY

Each raven had its own direction.
The he faced us,
the she turned away.
Each was a black moon
with one invisible side.
Together, they equaled front and back,
a whole shroud of feathers
twice as black
as one moon, one raven, one side.
We saw eyeballs roll back
like marbles.
The ball bearing of a retina
gleamed without stiffness or pride.

The beak of the one
who lets us see it
has been to the black ocean
and the white sun.
It has swallowed
truths and mice,
falsehoods and shining fish;
and it is hard
with its delicate touch
over the yellowest
kernel of corn.
It learned a wonderful joke
as it flew above the world,
but won't tell it here in this place
that hasn't one ocean or mountain.
Later, we climbed the black wall
of sex.
It was the raven

that made such strange noises
in our mouths.
It was the raven,
no longer captive,
flying inside us
with marble insistence,
with black and feathery
laughter.

## DETAILS FROM THE AUGUST HEAT: YOUR RAPE ONE YEAR LATER

The unripe tomato left to sun
on the garbage can lid, the tight
yellow wax of its waiting, the gourd pitched
sideways, unbalanced, its sickly green
looks weakened, the color of a lime
held under water. Slick with August dew,
this day must also begin for you.

One year ago today, you woke, in darkness,
to a new, less complicated life. A knife
at your throat, a man unbalanced, slick
with that addiction: not to you,
but to your life, submerged, blurred
beyond all recognition. Not to you,
but for your absolute, unwavering attention.

Tiger lilies have a way of hiding out
against garage doors, brick walls, or a gray
fencepost. My old landlord keeps them for his wife,
dead three years. To whom he sings each night,
playing badly on the mandolin. Music
is at least a fan: the sorrow pushes
at a curtain, touches a face, rearranges the invisible

helpless air. "Well, now you'll have
something to write about," that young man said, then
raped you. "Details," you wrote me once,
"those are the things which can be said,
huge and neglected." The next day
you left that place for good. You found a house
with double locks, a yard, a suburb far away.

And then the nights began to make you pay.
Terror is boring, each night the same ritual:
he is back inside the house, making his way slowly,
cut by cut, into your waiting life. You are certain
that you will always wake like this, forced
to be what he must have, again and again. His face
will never end. His jittery way with words. His steady,
gloved hands.

The old man has a secret: water
every night after dark. A pool of black water
under each stake. He says
that's what it takes for tomatoes *like this*:

he makes a circle gesture meaning perfect.
*Perfect* is a full night's sleep.
You will lean up against it, a gray fencepost,

and one night it will hold.
This day waits for you, huge
and neglected. You will not forget
where you have been and what was done
upon you. Details from the August heat:
grapes ease their way from green to purple, you
work all day then turn to childrens' stories.

*Once upon a time*, the large print reads,
and the words glide by
like illustrated days in a bedtime fairytale.

# IV
## BLACK & WHITE / COLOR

## A SUDEK PLACE
*on a photograph by Josef Sudek*

Here's a Sudek place:
an empty park, the curved
wave of a wooden bench
in sunlight, beached
among the fallen leaves.
When waiting, watching,
silence, patience
are the games, then Sudek
loves to play and play.
Mostly, it's the wall
of sunlight that first
attracts. But, then,
the bench, each wooden
slat a longed-for curve
no one knows they want
until they see it here,
in autumn, in
Sudek's photograph.

A Sudek place is
always free and
open to the public;
a church, say, or
a leaf, an egg on a
plate, or the way
a hat sits in sunlight
at a picnic.
All this shows why Sudek
never married.
He took the whole world

in sickness and in health.
He never betrayed
leaf, egg, hat, dusk.
And the bench knew —
like an arched wave, like a
new bride — that with Sudek
as groom, there was always
someone to provide.

# THE VALLEY CALLED CURVE
### Josef Sudek, photographer (1896–1976)

Say you think too much; and say you think
in squares: airless, sharp, all too clear.

Sudek says: you need an egg. He placed
them everywhere a border got too tight.

He made the edges disappear. He
made sharp things curve, he took an oval

and anchored it in space. He displayed the egg
upright and speckled; then, he photographed;

then, ate. Later, he snapped the plate
and leftover, broken shell. The remains

photographed well: lacework on a plate,
a million fragments. An egg is a seal,

flipperless and still, a helpless
lump filled to the brim with shape.

An egg is a seal placed in the glistening
valley called *curve*. Sudek says: place it

by bread that's been nibbled and stood on its crust.
Watch, he says, how food regresses into stuff,

kingdoms where we live by shape alone,
and each object calls to Sudek with the

same absolute attention a mourner has
for the last look at a corpse's face.

Sudek says: never torment yourself.
He sets up a glass of beer, and lays

the fresh and everpresent egg against it.
The glass beads like a curtain. Carefully,

Sudek counts beads for us in the eye
of the camera. We learn to see them

one by one, as well as the curtain of glass,
and the valley that curves away, beyond the curtain.

## HERE, TOO, THERE IS A PARADISE
### on a photograph of Prague by Josef Sudek

If the city has a bridge, he loves it
in black and white. Streetlamps and statues line
the Charles Bridge side by side. The old tide
of night is coming in, rising in gray
streaks off the river. Each statue is a saint
face on. As if swept bare of people,
the bridge stands pure and expectant.
Colors are not permitted in Sudek's world,
are unforgiven for their gorgeous pandering
to reality. This is something else. Here,
in this landscape of black and white, here, too,

there is a paradise. As Prague approaches
night, each black shape on Sudek's contact sheet
calls to the other. This is what love is
on a bridge: the dark of one shape calling
to the dark of another. Streetlamps, saints: all
the smudged and haunted ones. Sudek searches
his city for the moment when gray sings
to gray, and river to bridge; when all things
resemble one another just enough
for statues of saints to light our way
like streetlamps, and for streetlamps to speak
to God like saints, with the gray light of unlit
glass faces. It is almost too dark to see
the clouds above Sudek's Prague, where already
night moves among the restless, unfalling rain.

## ROTHKO

He saw the gray on black, and that
was that. Two shapes of dark
came at him, parted, waited.
Shapes had been like chairs before.
He could always rest in a shape.
Before the gray came,
every oblong was a way to say the world,
a pitched tent of color in the wild
and arbitrary forest of all our longings.
He even found his own Matisse,
his homage, in oblongs, like a window
thrown open on yellow and orange, on patterns
that only the casual eye, lazy with joy, can find.
Sometimes he dreamt the world pastel,
dreamy curtains of color he hung
over bars of light, and left to be opened.
But he couldn't drench the black.
So, he painted what he owed it: square
after square. He gave the black
that final gray, a last oblong weight,
the simple and furious grave above the black,
the last place he had to go to paint. It was
hardly dry, but he went in to stay, inside
the shape he had made himself of himself.

## MATISSE'S "DANCE"

Nothing we do will ever be as free as this:
outflung bodies tipped towards blue sky
like ecstatic toasts about to be drunk
by an earth that can barely contain them.
Never looking back, the women clasp hands
as they dance, scatter the invisible air
with buttocks and backs, sheen-black hair, unclasped
and comely as Stravinsky's sad Petrouchka, freed
at last and laughing. They're never going back
to clothes, to elastics that force stomachs flat
or rein in breasts; nor to gravity
that weighs us down like sacks of wasted flesh.
The unresistant green of a painted,
slippery grass lets them leap as if the earth
is a trampoline, a paradise
of jump and whirl and touch. Up close, we see
green paint streaks their legs like a spring rain.
It leaves a careless, splashy wake, an ex-
huberant trail of jagged, squiggly clues:
this is the dance of those with nothing to lose.
They go round and round, splashed with paint,
and covered all over with a thick coat
of pleasure. So absorbed in the wild fling
of their bodies, their lowered faces
are solitary, monastic, filled
with the godly pinks of shiny flesh
defying gravity on the trapeze
of its dance. No net, no pole, no need
for balance at all. We who remain grounded,
bench-bound, watch their flesh shine, delicious
sowing of blue leaps, green robes of cut grass
channeled in a flow of color deep enough

for us to drown in. We who breathe
must have these small deaths by color, leaning
as far as we can into the river
of pure astonishment. We hoped
paradise would be like this, so much green
spilled into blue, everything unbuttoned
from gravity, naked, dancing hand in hand.

# V
## TERROR'S ONLY EPITAPH

# TERROR'S ONLY EPITAPH

On December 29th, 1975, a bomb exploded at La Guardia airport
in New York in the baggage area. Scores of people were killed or
seriously hurt. No one ever took "credit" for the bomb; the guilty
person was never found. At the time of the explosion I was wait-
ing for a plane one floor up and a little to one side of where the
bomb went off.

I

I saw how it was with the living.
All the sudden conversations,
little spurts of talk
springing up like campfires
at which we warm our hands:
"Three dead?" "Three,
hell. Twelve at last count,
and still digging."
"My God.
My God."
The words
keep us warm.
We never give our names
as we talk.
We all have one name:
*survivor*,
and each word we say
is an added degree of warmth taken
from the raging fire
those twelve voices
lit for us.
A blue light in an ambulance.
Like a grotto blue in a da Vinci

it is the center around which
death huddles.
Again and again, the ambulances come.
The blue lights shine, add
darkness after darkness
to their glow.

A young boy sits on the hood of a car
in the parking lot.
A bag of Christmas presents is at his side.
He cries, and is ashamed.
He bends his head to the sack
to hide his tears.

We found taxis, did knee bends,
ate grapefruit. I saw that it was easy
to go home: the arms
of a lover held me tighter
than all the arms of the twelve dead.
It was easier
to see the dawn of the next morning
than to stay one more second
in that broken night.
It was easier
to return home
than to stay a stranger
among the dead.
It was simpler to speak
the old language of the living,
than to learn the bloated
and indistinguishable syllables
of those whose mouths
are full of dirt.

## II THE DEAD ONES SPEAK

Try to see how it was.
We've just walked down some stairs for our baggage.
We're thinking of the trip around the world about to begin,
or of the next painting we want to do,
or we work for the Long Island Limousine Company
and we've come to pick up the bags of arriving passengers.
We are chatting, we grunt under the bags' heaviness,
secretly we curse all weight.
Or we are remembering the left hand corner
near the frame where we might put in a dab of black.
We are not forgetting the suit that must be pressed,
nor the course we almost failed,
nor the orange dress that packs so well.
We think of that old teacher who died in Mexico last year,
and the raise we didn't get.

Something was just on the tip of our tongue
when glass— which had been so smooth,
which had always opened before our touch,
which had given us light
and through which so much world had entered us
as we stood at windows or lay back with the shades up—
when glass which had never spoken a word before
enters our ear with a little whisper.
Or it speaks to our throat
and our head sails across the baggage area
(like a baseball, says a witness later)
or it pushes everything it has against our face
which hides in a thousand places
and won't come out and isn't ever completely found
before the funeral.
Or there's a large hole in our jacket (how did *that* get there)

where once there had been a stomach.
Our bodies became a kind of rubbish.
Here a hand, there a shoe, here a head,
there a hat. We had no plan
at the moment of our deaths.
Don't try to say we were brave,
we never had time for that.
Don't try to say we were special,
we were ordinary as breath.
"Heart sickening," a survivor said later
of what was left of us. Heart-
sickening is the only epitaph.

## III IN THE EVOLUTION OF TERROR

At first,
when a universe is created,
God has too much to do.
There are already widows
who must be comforted.
There are wedding rings
without any fingers
because the bang that created
this universe spared rings
but not fingers.
It preserved metal
but let the flesh go,
brushed it off peoples' bones
like lint.
It was casual,
this bomb —
without pretense
or false politeness.
It took a druggist,
an artist,
an old woman.
It specialized only
in drivers of limousines:
three.
In the beginning,
God invented the parking lot.
A universe of concrete,
of people milling in small groups,
of fist fights over who used the telephone,
the one telephone
God had installed
in his parking lot.

In the evolution of disaster
many strange creatures appeared:
ambulances with blue lights
revolving in their white interiors,
sirens that never stopped
and men in blue uniforms
guarding the new universe
with drawn guns.
But the strangest creature of all
is the dead.
God invented the dead,
12 silent and unyielding disciples,
before he invented dying.
He gave them their deaths
before he taught them how to die.
And then God rested.

# VI
## GIVING AWAY LOVE

## DO SEE IT MY WAY

Something new and different, something you.
Like the white puff of a moon
after the sun has come up; the you.
Wind in the palms after rain passes, the salty
and somewhat foreign smell of you.
Or, as the kids say, she's rough, meaning
she's smooth as we used to say, or tough, or cool;
she's you. To make love is to wish
on the first star. Like sunlight
on water, it may or may not go deeper,
may or may not come true.

I am not ready to be
your total seriousness, your everything.
Your any little thing
will do. Like soap on skin,
that bubbling pleasure; or the joke
about the pig with the wooden leg, just any
little thing. In the seeming as much
as the is. In the jay trailing its blue wing
through the fog. In the sudden impulse to touch you,
there and there.

It will be at least as lonely
with as without you, but more flex time
in certain intimate moments. How ridiculous
the effort, how staggered the shocked
and uncertain step, the brave
and pudgy knees of all desire. Do
continue slowly, one lovely knee
at a time. Do see it my way.

In the first wine, there is joy;
in the new moon, the boast
to darkness. So beautiful rings,
so music and candlelight
can give the brooding universe
its wings, its looseness, its handhold
on flickering and play.
*Hush*, say the warming ones:
silence, wish to wish. It takes two
to be you and me. Ebb and flow
in the deep waters, a bit of yes,
a bit of no. Maybe some apricot-blonde
tree blossoms to light the way
through late afternoons.
You will or you won't,
who knows? The pleasure
of being alone:
anticipation is the only limit.
You will be
the shape of what is, a definite
way of leaning forward
in an uncomfortable orange chair,
laughing, holding back,
giving in.

## IN RAIN

Only the gray cat crossing the silver of an empty street.
Only the pigeon picking at its breast,
fascinated with the perpetual itch of its own body.
Only sex in front of the fireplace, the old
hesitations, the flames a blur
of creamy light on the ceiling;
only the flickering cream of heat, once removed.
Only the me and the you, the thorn and the rose, the hurt
still falling and falling though the cat is easy
and swell, its tail tipped in white.
The how of its stroll through the sky's dripping
is only one truth, but I want it. The fur
slicked back along my body. And the naked.
And the who that glitters within its bullet-shaped head.
It is only the sex. But I want it. And the how and the who
of the world's tears falling everywhere at once
and me the one with the red tongue, rough,
a rippled muscle drinking, only drinking
at the trough of the sky's fallen body, those tears,
                    that sweat, our rain.

## THAT'S THE DUSK

So many dusks like this
when I've stood facing
the blue after-life
of daylight, the cello-
moan of purple scraping
the trees. Darkness,
the one I love,
is coming. Not the black
of full night: that's too much
shyness. But when you
stand by a window
looking out at the birdhouse,
the tips of your fingers
against your cheek and the light
leaving your hair strand
by strand; then, a glistening
pool of shadows forms
above your head: that's
the dusk that lets me in.

## WHAT THE BIRD SEES

You rise up in the darkness,
over my body.
The white necklace at your throat,
the balls of ivory around your neck.
You open
your water-lily flesh
high up the side of the mountain in its own pond,
swaying, unafraid.
The blossoms rise small and tight
out of the green lips of the palmy leaves.

Need has found its breasts and entered them.
You invite me;
the leaves of your blooming are wide and wet.

The motionless bird on the chimney flies up.
It saw something there in the distance,
maybe another blackness like itself,
maybe the soft curl of sticks and hay woven in the circle of
                    a nest.
The weave of darkness, the ivory beads, the sticks and hay
of our mingling breaths. We saw what the bird sees
and bore up our separate wings to that waiting nest.

## GIVING AWAY LOVE

Since morning it's been raining on the sea,
since morning it's been graying. Herons
scrape slow shadows across the flats.

There are eyelashes in the morning, little feathers
of seagrass caught between rain and the saltier rain
of the sea. I am darker than the rest, and dry

like wood under a tarp being saved for the fire.
The truest dreams have rain for faces, have surf
for their long rolling bodies. They don't wake,

they are dignified and a little crazy. They
rarely stray this way, so close to waking.
But since morning it's been raining on the sea.

I say that I'm dry, but I'm on the edge:
a little balcony with an overhang, feet wet,
barely awake, giving love away.

Inside the room behind me, still
in darkness, sleeps the woman I love, a dream
away, before us the slowly forming day.

I'm giving love to the sea, a wing, some grasses.
Giving it to rain, and that shifting, wind-drenched
gray. Giving it to dreams I can't remember

and a certain dryness: this flimsy body something
lives in called "I". Giving love a flowering and a need:
since morning it's been raining on the sea.

## LONDON: 33, THE LAST MOVEMENT,
## THE LONGEST DAY

1

He was thirty-three for the last time.
It was late afternoon and he'd seen the tailor
on the museum's wall with his black scissors and row
of perfect buttons. Then he'd gone to the large room
with the awful reds and sunsets laminated pink
and stared at The Four Stages of Man
and their objects: toy, guitar, armor, money.

Each stage was gloomy, and so, to cheer himself
he stopped in room 24 at the laughing cow
in the della Francesca, its mouth gigantic with blue
in the otherwise dignified and eerie whites
of the nativity scene. It was London, June '77,
late afternoon of the year's longest day and his last chance
in the old year to stand next to a cow belly-
laughing with joy at the virgin birth.

The deaths of Christ in the medieval pictures are silver,
a moon of flesh stretched across the canvas, light
by which to see the world bathed in death, the staked planet
of the body on the cross: orbiting god
of deep crevices, dark side, valleys and mountains.

2

It was 5pm when he left the museum
to walk a while in the gray light of St.Martin's Street
past the sidewalk portrait painter. The man
who was barely 33 thought of the gauze on those christs
of the 14th century, the translucent silver cloths,
the dead penis under its gauzy map of the crotch's wilderness.

Every few feet he stopped and made a painting in the air
of what he saw before him: lovers standing
by a trash basket kissing until the news vendor
who also sells concertinas turns away.

The man walking alone on the eve of his 34th year
ate his cold green pepper,
drank scotch and coffee at the place where the Woman
Who Sits Alone dines in the splendor
of her notebook, pen, and books spread across the table.
If only she knew it was his last day on earth at this age,
maybe she would turn from her dreamy pause, pen in hand,
to answer the many questions for women he has formed
at this and all his unknowing ages.

3
He has chosen for his last evening at 33 the concert
of Beethoven's last sonatas, four shells
washed up on the last shore
where those forms that gave his life shelter
broke with the passion of age and regret.

The man in the concert hall didn't want to put the shells
                to his ear
for fear he would only hear the echo of his own longing.
But there it was, faint at first, the ocean,
that deep wind-entangled water of our birth,
those first floating bars of the opus 101A major
that depart so quietly from the silence which precedes them.

The man has known since 4 p.m. that he is trapped
in armor, life's Third Stage, head
propped up by hands at the painter's insistence

on the truth of posture, of a body inside armor
where shades of gray metal frame the exposed flesh of the face.

This man who is losing his year at last
is able to find the music of Beethoven's last years
by the final sonata's final chord
in that solitary moment when the pianist is ash gray
as the flesh of the thieves on either side of Christ.
In that silence when the player's fingers tremble over
                    the keys for the last time
and do not move again into the ivory flesh of
                    the instrument's body
the man who has been completing all day the portrait
of his visit to the kingdom of thirty-three
relinquishes it into the open palms, the wild
applause for this final, difficult, and unfinished music.

# VII
## FOR YOU

## FIRES THAT WON'T GO OUT

In Boston, the Vietnamese
are busboys. Their bodies
are long; tall as us.
They all wear sweaters
like college kids on a Friday night
in fall. But they are different;
thinner, and the color
won't let us go: a yellow
without wheat;
not an ounce of sun,
but a stalk in October
after harvest when the heat
still holds the split stalk.
Hours pass, as we eat
the cream sauce and drink white wine.
They are so tall
that they stoop, apologize
constantly with their bodies.
They bow their heads, jerk their arms
back and forth across the tables
like spiders. The nervous thread
of their net is money, the need
for warmth, for a country
of intelligible speech. These men
in sweaters— especially the one in twisted red,
the wool like strands of coral
smeared with sunlight—
have such anxious eyes.
Coals seem to burn
in the grates of their retinas.
There are fires that won't go out.

They fill the glasses at a glance from us.
They clean plates; bow like priests, and move
discreetly through our litter. The transformation
of our bodies into saviours
goes on all evening long
before their tired and wary eyes.

## ALL THE RAISED ARMS

The city wanders in spirals
from market to cathedral, from museum
to gutter, from cafe to postcard.
It takes its time and it pauses
at the flapping blue laundry, it puffs
its pipe at the signpost: the Divine Lily
is coming! Who will return
Lost Kitty of 8/15? The gray eyes
of the steeples are always so calm.
Part of the sky is a forehead
and part is the vague gesture
of an old man who lost his hair
and has walked all the way to the edge of the city,
crawled over the stone fence and separated
carefully the weeds from the flowers.
He puts the bouquet by her name in the little cemetery.
It is blue in the sky where his old hair
has blown far off in a corner. Someone took
a wheelbarrow and gave it to a little boy
right this minute, right now. He turns
its wheel with the pure exhaustion
of his play. He is moving silver
to the castle behind his mother's table.
His shirt is blue. Two tourists
have been given noon, a paper bag
with cheese, bread, and a little butter under a chestnut tree
full of the dust of Europe. Bells, wings, the worm
of a day is catching a quick nap behind the white
                    grandmother curtains
of the house on the right. And that silly bimbo of a grocer
has gone off again with his rolled sleeves and his bottle
looking for God knows what along the path behind the convent.

The spiral turns inside the rolled newspaper of the housewife.
She is looking for flies who have dared to invade
her kitchen. All the raised arms,
the stifled yawns, the winks.
All the open mouths demanding their bread
and singing their songs. All
the years that marbles have crashed against each other
inside the circle by the school. Not one is lost,
not one. Even the headmaster turns
and stands by his window to watch the game
and is not lost.

## THIS PASSING

The man is dying from cancer at thirty.
His hair is brown and curly,
he wears a shirt with blue around the sleeves.
He eats lentil soup
and speaks of Africa,
Guatemala— the trips a life can bring.
Already, the first year of his death
he has motorcycled west and back.
Now he's at a party, spooning soup, dying.
Ireland? Maybe Greece in May  . . .
The hostess is a close friend.
When he told her, she said, "No, no,"
and cried. For days she could do nothing else
but remember him before he spoke— how they canoed
far back into the Boundary Waters. Because of him
she was not afraid. She even swam naked
as long as he was near. Why must he tell her
such news about himself? She feels grief, yes. Sadness;
but, anger, too, at the almost casual voice
that counts himself out. He sees all this pass across her face
and feels guilty for his death. But there is no place
                        to leave it,
no parking space far enough away. It is awkward,
this passing of his. And so he offers to help his hostess—
                        his friend—
with her party, with the small arrangements for her life.
He takes candles out of the box
and twists them stick by stick into the diamond crevices
of cut glass. The smooth wax under his fingers,
then the fire. It's like a church, he says to himself.
Maybe I should see Notre Dame in Spring?
The poor neighbors.

They thought I was lazy when I quit my job.
If the candle on the right goes longest,
I'll last six months. If the candle on the left, twelve.
He forgets to look before he leaves.

In Mexico, in the museum of anthropology,
are the bodies from before Christ.
Nobody was laid out flat with a carnation plunged in
                                     a buttonhole;
no smiles were placed across the lips like drawn knives.
The living put each body sideways, a slight curve,
a fetus on its second journey.
The spines were like fishhooks
shaped to catch the first rush of the new world.

He is trying to say:
*I'd like to see that,*
*that's what I want to see.*
I believe, he says, the body's curve
at death is a hook for something larger.
I know the doctors think my hopes are only typical
for this stage. I know how hard they try
for truths that will fit themselves into instruments.
But the rule should be:
whoever is dying gets to have the first truth about himself.
And if I want to fall asleep under a giant pine in Georgia—
like the one in bootcamp that took four of us to stand around
fingertip to fingertip— I will. Because sleep is as true as
                                     I need to be
now, passing the raw white lights of the filling station
here in St.Paul, where everyone I can see is alive.

Tomorrow I check in again. Janie is the nurse who has trained
                     to work with us.

She has learned not to be surprised at how alive
               my chest looks.
Medication is a river that will never reach the sea.
Janie, my mother is dead. Thank God.
The father I hunted with on the Mississippi near the delta
knows nothing of this new death. I must speak to him.
I must tell him of my new desire
for Greece in May. No, what I really want to say is,
               "I loved it
when we read newspapers together in the living room,
handing each other our finished sections,
placing the papers carefully on each other's knees."
This medicine is hard to follow.
Who has any idea where it leads: river, sea, Greece?

## THE POET OF MINSK *(Russia, 1928)*
### In memory of Mandelstam and the others


The ice is melting in Minsk. Mid-March, the smell of black
               earth,
ice-stars under the streetlamps. There is a certain tree
on a certain corner where the buds open before all others.
The poet of Minsk knows this and much else.
What it means, for example, to love streetlamps,
which coffeehouse you can sit in for hours undisturbed,
which secret police (they follow him now day and night)
allow him to dangle on a longer rope, will let him
enter a store without following closely.
His friends weep for him. They forget whole lines of his poems.
It is hard being the most joyful man in Minsk. He sees laundry,
               squirrels
on the dead tree, Spring like a velvet tam on the end of his
               fingertips.
Why settle for one year at a time! He looks at the old man on
               the corner
and becomes what he sees. He turns toward the angle of roof
               beam,
where the pigeons roost. He is a pigeon, a roof, a beam, a dark
               strip
of pigeon world. He is a dead man. He knows that.
He is the only statistic in Minsk that stands alone.
No one who loves to murder would pass him up.
It is a beautiful night,
says the man who was pigeon, old man, piece of rotting wood;
a night like all the rest, wonderfully like all the rest.

## BEYOND THE BORDER

On the bus they sing, the people
who go from one place to another.
                              First,
the children, little blonde, little dark hair
and the boy towards the back in his white tee shirt:
*First comes the doctor,*
*then comes the nurse,*
*then comes the woman*
*with the alligator purse.*
The young man behind us leans forward,
"Well, it's been quite a day. I picked up the paper
and read about the forest fire; then I proposed to my girl
in Wisconsin." All of us lean back
and look out the window: a lake filled with the quilted gray
of dusk and the green light and blue streaks
which slowly stain the green into black
past Grand Marais, past Little Marais,
past the alligators rolling their logs soundlessly
in the long night of a child's sleep in her mother's arms.

At the border we pause
since one of us is from Hong Kong.
He has brought speakers, a tuner, the whole works
of music this long distance. The inspector looks
into the tight-woven fiber of the speakers.
But it's just cloth:
no green seaweed from the Gulf of Shamar has been trapped
                              inside;
no shells, no sand, no Chinese eels from the Bay of Sintar.
As he leaves the bus, the man from Customs is applauded.
When we move on into Canada we pass
a prison blindingly lit from within.

At each doorway there is a light,
as if someone had dropped something small and valuable
and were looking for it everywhere on hands and knees.
Quickly, the darkness returns
and we look straight ahead a long moment
into the relief of what can't be seen.

A factory appears, strings of light along its black
                              metal bones
like a Christmas tree broken into pieces
and left sprawling in the smoke-filled night.
Again, singing;
first from the two young women behind us,
the tuneless music that begins near sleep,
near arrival; without meaning
yet full of comfort.
We enter the city to the sound of human voices
moving back and forth through the other
thicker and repeated twang of the motor.
All of us with our little hums,
each black shadow in its seat,
each voice a spoke
inside the larger wheel
of our borderless journey,
together
for these last few miles.

## FOR YOU

I know it sounds too much like poetry,
but it was dusk that made me a felon,
a winter evening in Moline, Illinois.
The next day I quoted Whitman
to my draft board, "Dismiss
whatever insults your own soul,"
and sent my draft card back to them.
I can still feel the cold metal
on the mailbox, see the park
with its oaks, the black winter sky
so close, so distant,
as I dropped the letter inside
and turned quickly away.

For two years I'd argued the War,
drinking instant coffee with a man
who wore the same blue velour shirt so often
it's all I remember of him now.
We took turns arguing one way,
then another about "what to do."
We sat in the basement kitchen
of a boarding house.
Sometimes we yelled,
sometimes we sat silently, our hands
around our mugs of coffee,
our hearts confused. Deferments
from the draft meant we were the men
who could afford to choose a future.
And we had so wanted to go on drifting,
floating on the moment's shifting current
as we learned to give the poems we tried to write
a chance to rise, waveringly,

into their own shapes, existences
born of dreams, not arguments. I didn't want
to chant slogans. I didn't want
to be "right." To judge.
And these were more than choices,
these were entire lives, futures
that could never be redeemed —
or so we felt then in the midst
of a slaughtering time.
Back and forth we went, the guy
in the blue velour shirt and I,
all of us who read Emerson and Thoreau,
ate frozen dinners, drank
3.2 beer, played pinball or pool —
any game at all that would give us
a few hours away from ourselves,
those of us who underlined
CIVIL DISOBEDIENCE and wrote excited comments
in the margins late at night,
rather than actually take to the streets.

I lived alone in Moline, Illinois,
one dusty and dimly lit flight
above a greeting card shop
run by a likeable red-faced
John Bircher. It was the first year
I got paid for teaching, paid
for being excited
about what I believed in,
for having opinions
I couldn't give away
to my friend in the velour shirt.
Then two students quit school
and within months were dead

in Vietnam. A working class
college, our basement classroom
was in an old pentecostal church.
The mix of Sunday School
and poverty was too much
on Monday mornings, the students
almost asleep, sprawled
on the freshly waxed floors,
huddled near their classrooms
like refugees waiting for their morning soup
rather than for classes to begin.

I was the razzle dazzle guy
from the Big U
in Iowa City. I didn't
own a tie, I lived
in a VW bus all fall,
I had opinions that gave off
the glitter of newly minted
funny money. To the students
I was a classy eccentric
and I had them with me from the first,
those future postal clerks
and nurses, mechanics
and would-be writers
with their mixed bag of Sartre
and letter jackets, hickeys
and acid and— finally—
of life and death.

The second student who died
had sat in the back of the room,
chair tilted against the wall,
his long hair spread out behind him

like a scraggly fan. He often
brought his guitar to class
in a black case, and wrote his poems
on cheap yellow paper. He wanted
to know about mileage
from my bus: these
were the only details I remembered
when his girlfriend told me he had been killed.

It was winter by then
and I was living alone
above the greeting card shop.
After that second student's death
I spent the week-end by myself.
I was reading Suzuki at the time
and wanted to believe in something,
even if it was only the pull
and release of my own breath
as I sat cross-legged, meditating
best I knew how. I liked Zen.
For someone raised an Anglican
it seemed the closest thing
to all that upper class tastefulness, so
lovely, so earnest in its own careful way.
While I sat, meditating, I felt
even lonelier: all my enthusiasm
in the classroom, my voluble
and spontaneous love of poetry
that fit itself so nicely
into the 50 minute school hour,
my a la mode hiking boots.
I thought of that dead boy
with his guitar and his questions,
and the careful but wasted economy

of his cheap yellow paper
and I felt sick to my soul,
for all my talk of Thoreau and Whitman.
I wanted to be a citizen again, to Pledge
Allegiance to something with the faith
I'd felt in 4th grade, facing
the flag behind Miss Rodger's desk.
It was my country, too,
not just the John Bircher's downstairs
with his saccharine greeting cards
and his private gun collection.

That weekend I drank green tea,
believing it more Japanese than Lipton Orange.
I stared at the gray clouds
of dust under the bed, I followed
the flow of my breath
in and out of my stomach—
like a golden river, Suzuki said.
For two days I did nothing
but alternately sit and then hobble
on legs permanently sore
from being crossed so much.
I quit thinking about everything: the draft,
my dead students,
the future, the past. Was it
a spiritual state? I don't know,
but I felt as if I'd grown 3 inches overnight
and everything I saw
looked slightly different,
smaller and further away,
the way a dream does
as you wake up
and it begins to leave you.

99

Towards evening of the second day
I'd had enough of the hush,
pause, hush, of my own breath
and the shooting pain of ankles
and knees. I wanted out
and away from those motionless dust balls.
It felt wonderful to walk into evening
alone in Moline, Illinois,
in the middle of America,
the weightless center
of a centerless country.

I walked and I looked.
I saw some men sitting at a bar.
I stood outside, staring
through the small pane of glass
at the top of the door.
Everything moved so slowly:
my breath still deep
and even, holding me rooted
in the evening air like an anchor
when men fish from a boat and seem to drift,
but are only rocking back and forth
between one known place and another.
I saw the men, heads bent
toward the neon light of a beer sign
behind the bar: a man with a lasso
in one hand and a beer in another.
The lasso was red, the beer golden.
A bartender stood beside the sign,
white-aproned, holding a pencil.
I watched as he gestured
towards the bent heads of the men
sitting before him. One of them

nodded up and down and that simple,
barely noticeable sign of agreement
brought tears to my eyes
and an assent of my own
where I stood anchored
by my own steady breath.
I walked on, went up the hill
that rose steeply away from the river
near where I lived. A sled
had been left out for the night
on a front yard's thin crust of snow.
I saw this ordinary sight
framed in a deepening gray
like a letter in a phrase,
still undeciphered, but so important
that once I understood it
it would change the meaning of all other words.

As I walked slowly up the hill,
other objects I saw seemed part
of the same phrase:
a porch swing drawn up on its two chains
waiting near the roof for spring;
a car with a broken windshield
glittering under a streetlight
like the traces of a phosphorescent map;
the corner of an old newspaper
frozen into an iced-over sidewalk.

"For you," I found myself saying
over and over as I neared the top of the hill.
My breath came in short gasps now,
"For you, for you."
It became a kind of greed.

I couldn't get enough
of the men with their bent heads in the bar,
the sled, the swing. They gave
and I took.
I wanted it to go on forever,
this greed for the world. I knew
that it was for the sake of a sled
left behind in the moment of impatience
for dinner that I would go to prison.
Not just for political reasons,
not even for moral ones:
not for reasons at all,
or not the kind I could explain
to a draft board. For you,
sled. For you, bent heads.
For you, for you.

If, in a moment of peace, the world
could yield up such signs,
then I wanted an inner peace,
both permanent and casual.
But I could not begin
until I settled with the War.
It was that dusk, that walk, that sled
that convinced me their world could sustain me
if only I could abandon my soul-searching
and endless arguments over what to do,
like a character in a Chekhov story
so busy talking outside
on a cold winter's night
he almost dies of frostbite
while trying to prove the existence of God.

If it meant going to prison,
so be it. There, too, there would be
ordinary sights that would sustain me.
Or so I told myself
in that moment when I believed so deeply
in the strangely calming power
that came from seeing clearly
into the heart of everyday life.
I stood at the top of the hill, alone,
surrounded by what I loved.
I looked down towards the Mississippi,
black except where a bridge curved
through the night, and I did not know
what the future would bring
or what it was inside me
that would not let go
of my two new words, "For you."

Jim Moore is the author of *The New Body* (University of Pittsburgh Press), *What The Bird Sees* (Momentum Press), and *How We Missed Belgium* (in collaboration with Deborah Keenan, Milkweed Editions). In addition, he was co-editor, with Cary Waterman, of *Minnesota Writes: Poetry*, an anthology (Milkweed Editions, 1987). His work has been widely published in magazines and anthologies, and he is the recipient of several fellowships and awards for both his prose and his poetry. He lives in St. Paul, Minnesota, and teaches writing at The Minneapolis College of Art and Design. He is married to the photographer JoAnn Verburg. Jim Moore has recently completed a book of personal essays.